Three Walled World

POETRY

Three Walled World
Copyright © 2026 by Ellery Capshaw
Cover by: Michael J. Seidlinger
ISBN: 9781960988881 (paperback)

CLASH Books
Troy, NY
clashbooks.com
Distributed by Consortium
All rights reserved.
First Edition: 2025

No part of this book may be reproduced in any form or by any electronic or mechanical means, including information storage and retrieval systems, without written permission from the author, except for the use of brief quotations in a book review.

Praise for Ellery Capshaw

"In *Three Walled World*, Ellery Capshaw takes us behind the scenes of her childhood, where she has the gift to 'chameleon into any name, any experience that lived between lines.' This tender, haunting memoir defies genre, and transports us to childhood bedrooms, daybreak car rides, inedible feasts, and the bottom of an empty bottle, perfecting her performance while we watch her discover that there's no script for the grief we feel right alongside her."

— **Lisa Mangini author of *Ambivalent Nymph***

"Ellery Capshaw's *Three Walled World* is a memoir-in verse that confronts grief head-on. It is an elegy for a lost father and lost childhood. Retracing Capshaw's own experience of being a child actor on a long-running Soap, the book's personal narrative opens unto philosophical questions. With its piercingly honest voice, Capshaw's debut will stay with you, long after you close the book."

— **Shara McCallum, author of *Madwoman* and *Behold***

"Subdued yet incisive, *Three Walled World* reveals the complex interior of a girl growing up in the glow of the studio lights, navigating grief, visibility, and self-invention. Capshaw writes with a tenderness sharpened by truth."

— **Stephanie Valente, author of *Internet Girlfriend***

"This is a moving, intimate debut that surprised me, challenged me, and lingered well beyond the final page. *Three Walled World* is a book you don't rush through—even when you can't put it down."

— **Alan Locher, *The Locher Room***

This collection is dedicated to my mother.
And my father: I'll write you poems until I run out of words.

Contents

ACT I	1
The Girl Who Found the End of the Earth	3
Open With:	4
The First Saturday Morning	6
My Weeks Became Nights	8
Hot Chocolate and Corn Muffins	10
Next Stop New York	12
Audition Diary 1	14
The Dancers	17
Audition Diaries 2	18
The Tenth Audition	20
ACT II	23
Drive to the E 14th Street Building	24
Natalie Snyder is:	26
Where the Stairs Go	29
Food on Set	30
Subway Grease	32
The Haircut	34
Dressing Rooms	37
Wardrobe	39
The Many Mothers	41
The Dollhouse	42
BLANK	45
Green Room	46
The Brat and Her Brother	48
On Lying	50
Intermission	53
The Seven Things My Father Is	54
Act III	59
Answers to Questions I Never Had	60
How to Come Back to Life	62
I Remember the Years After like Falling	64
The Dream Where I Drown	66

The Feeling of Things	68
My Mother	70
On Google Searching	73
How Endings are Also Beginnings	74
My Father, My Natalie, My Memory	77
Even now, When I Close My Eyes, I Can See Her	78
Cover Charge	80
The National Institute on Drug Abuse Says 50% of My Addiction is Genetics	83
How to Celebrate the Dead	84
Five Years and Four Days After I First Said I Needed to Stop Drinking, I Did	86
My Father Has Been Dead for Sixteen Years & Last Night I Dreamt it Was a Lie	89
Acknowledgments	93
About the Author	95
Also by CLASH Books	97

Three Walled World
A Poetic Memoir

Ellery Capshaw

ACT I

The Girl Who Found the End of the Earth

It is hard to tell what will be real here.
There is a girl. Many girls within the girl.
The girl became so many girls she grew
   with no space to put them,
and she grew and grew until she was so many
   little girls, she popped.
Not like a helium balloon. Like a hose with a leak,
   spraying, struggling
to get water out of its metal mouth.
And the girl's parents never knew their hose
   was leaking because
the water still came out fine and it still grew the garden.
Her father, the jester, sang songs about nothing, built a swing
by the river for her. Taught her how to throw cooked noodles
to the wall. Whose car drove her so far, through all
   the Burroughs,
up to colder countries, around the corner and back again.
One day, the girl watched that car as it grew wings
and tried to find the end of the Earth. The car soared
and soared until her father chose the brake pedal instead.
Her mother, who still holds her when the leaks
spray, is the one, the only one, that survived it all.

Three Walled World

Open With:

```
second grade production of Annie.


A gaggle of giggling orphaned girls, tugging
at the hem of the Miss Hannigan-dressed
teacher, trying to keep time with the beats
of It's a Hard Knock Life. Scrubbing the
classroom-tiled floor with clean rags. In
the back row of the makeup smudged dirty
faces
```

Was me.
    In this moment, I have pigtails
    down to my waist; straight, straw hair
    my mother hated unknotting brushes from.
    I have spent the weeks before learning
    not just the five words I uttered in the center
    of the desk-cleared 'stage', but every word.
    I longed for the curly red-haired wig,
    the belt of longing for tomorrow.

    The way I remember it: I am flailing
    my second grade arms to a piano recording of *Annie*.
    I am spotlighted. There is a sound booth and my parents
    are in red velvet mezzanine seats and the stage is not
    a classroom but a grand theatre hall with crown molding
    catching gold in the stage lights' path.
  This is how the obsession started.
With memorizing,
    cloaking my seven-year-old
    self in as many different names,
                     words,
                     predicted emotions,
                     calculated movements

I could fit inside my small body.
I remember my parents being so impressed,
my father lifted me to his shoulders.
    And the feeling.
The feeling like I was some elementary-school starlet.
The high of pretending.

The First Saturday Morning

My father waves me in from my hiding place behind him and into the studio which is above a Planet Fitness gym. "This the acting class?" He asks the room. We're late, of course, and the man at the front of the room nods his head. My father closes the door, just hitting my back.

The vinyl floor of the dance studio feels like it drops off into a long, vortex hole that would swallow me if I took one more step. As if I could peer down, wonder how long the falling would be. Wonder what is swimming all the way down there.

I don't move. I say nothing and the rows of bent metal folding chairs look as if they are hanging in a mist. The heads all turn slowly, creaking as their necks snap into mechanical places. I am alone and the only child. I am seven and too young to be here but they let me anyway. And this all feels so scary and these people move nothing like real people. They all move in unison. And my father is gone and this is nothing like *Annie*.

This...this is when I start to cry. When the vinyl panels breathe back in and become floor again. The man with salt and pepper hair comes over to me. His tall, lean body makes me feel even smaller in the doorway. He introduces himself as Gary and says, "Why don't you take your coat off, take a seat." His smile wrinkles the sides of his eyes.

And I do. I drape my dalmatian-printed heavy coat on the ballet bar and walk slowly behind him. I sit in the bowl of a dent in a folding chair in the back row. My feet dangle off the edge as I wipe away tears. I say nothing for the two hours and no one says anything to me. I hang my head and listen to what scene books we need, monologues we'll need to memorize.

When it's over, I slide out of my seat, collect my jacket, and finally meet my father in the lobby.

"How'd it go kiddo," He asks me.

"It was fine, I guess," I huddle to the window and stay silent the whole car ride back.

Later that night, as I reach into the freezer after dinner, the phone rings. My mother answers, twirling the house phone cord between her fingers. "It's Gary," she says with one hand over the phone. I drop the pint of ice cream and close the freezer. I slump to the floor as their conversation continues. "Did you cry?" My mother asks me, concerned, while the call is still going. I nod my head while sitting on the kitchen floor. "Why?" Her voice is soft and sympathetic.

"It was scary, it's only old people and me," I tell her. Thinking I might cry again.

She lays the phone down on the counter and comes down to the floor and hugs me. "Do you want to go back?" She asks, stroking my hair. "Why don't you just try again. One more time?"

"Okay, one more time," I tell her.

She gets up, picks up the phone again. "She'll be back next Saturday," my mother returns the phone to the wall.

Three Walled World 7

My Weeks Became Nights

      cross-legged on my bed,
flipping through scenes.
      I memorized everything.
I said each word to myself
      a thousand times, Inflecting
different words. Made myself feel
      more anger, more sadness, more shock.

In those early years, I would learn
      every monologue in my library of books.
      Every, *monologues for girls, for teens, for teen girls,*
      for kids
      book there was, I owned it and I learned it.
I believed I could be anyone. I could chameleon
      into any name, any experience that lived between lines.

Gary would tell me my character   crosses stage left,
      then down to center,
   then behind the chair to right
and I would practice the route in my room,
   Three steps to the dresser,   five up to the edge
of my closet as my arms thrusted up, then down,
because, yes,   I was angry.

Over and over until I'd lay across my two
pushed together twin beds, under the draped
mosquito netting my father had hung up for me
like a princess, desperate for something she never
considers could be true. Until I believed
                              I made my own choices.

Hot Chocolate and Corn Muffins

Some Saturday mornings, Gary's two-door would pull into the driveway.
He'd pick me up before class and his car always had this smell.
Like cologne, like new car, like old car, like old books, like the end of wick.

                                          I haven't smelt it since.

I'd pile my scripts and folders on my lap as the automatic seatbelt
swung from the ceiling and across my chest. It was like being in a spaceship,
so fantastic, fun, and special.   It was special.

We'd pull into the parking lot of a pink and orange coffee shop
for a hot chocolate swirled with tall, whipped cream and a corn muffin.
It's glossy top at the bottom on a white paper bag.

Ellery Capshaw

Don't open it just yet, Gary would say as the car entered lunar
   take-off.
But still, I'd pick away at the crumbling top, crunch the
   toasted, sugary
edges and the crumbs would fall, clinging to the fleece of my
   jacket,
the static in the seatbelt, the short, curled fibers of the car floor.
Beneath the top, I could sponge the muffin between my fingers,
sculpt it into tall ridges, make fingerprint craters and watch as
the baked good slowly found its form again.

I'd help Gary arrange mangled folding chairs in rows,
trying to find the best one. The one without a dip
so large I'd be sitting in it as if it were a giant spoon.

No matter where the studio moved to, there would always be
9 a.m. classes, cottonmouth from too much coco, and crumbs
                              hiding in every crevasse.

Next Stop New York

Well, if you think she's so good, why don't you do it.
My mother says, bewildered when Gary tells her
I could really do this. I could really be something.
I stand in silence between them. It'd been two years.
And by then, I was disciplined. Looking up,
equally surprised, Gary steps back.
       Says he will.

The walls of a New York City agent's office
are plastered with photoshopped smiles of people I recognize.
The hall of movie posters
goes on for what feels like miles
until I stand tiptoed to see over
a woman's tall oak desk. I nervously
shake her hand, we meet and chat
and she hands me highlighted sides. Tells me
to read them. Gary, with both his thumbs up
in the corner, smiles his creasing smile as I read.

The way I've been taught to read: script at hips,
eyes barely glancing down to steal the words
in one swooping blink, chin up and eyes returning to her.
The calculations of a cold reading.
I drop the script to my side and she leans her head
back and forth, gently ushering me out of the room.
I sit on a chair that leaves my legs to kick the air and cling onto its seat.
Gary thanks her as he closes the door and waves me over.
We say nothing until we push open the front doors and the New York City
steam surrounds us. He lifts me under my arms,
you did it, you did it kiddo.
We celebrate with Ben & Jerry's that melts all over us,
not even the mountain of napkins we brought can stop
my fingers from sticking with melted mint chocolate.
We settle into pleather red and blue seats as Gary rattles off to my mother
about paperwork and signatures and how *it's really happening*.
I stare down, watching my ice cream slowly soup in my lap.

Audition Diary 1

The first audition I remember going on was for a movie. Well, an independent film. There was a hallway, lined with other children dangling their feet off metal chairs whispering lines to themselves, shuffling creased highlighted sides, moving their hands for emotion as flickering fluorescent bulbs sprayed green-tinted light. We were all pretending to be the same person. A sea of blonde-haired nine-year-olds with glossy headshot photos and resumes.

I wore a butterfly-bedazzled tank top bought at a boardwalk in Florida and ankle-length black cargo pants; an outfit pulled together by pink, chunky, dirt-stained sneakers. All the practicing spilled out of me in a blur of calculated memorization as a man behind a camcorder prompts me to begin. Did I breakdance during this audition? Yes. Did they ask me to breakdance? Probably not.

I booked it. It was called *Almont Now*. I can't find anything about it but I remember popping up from behind couches, side tables, curtains and saying the same line over and over. The set was part studio space, part vacant building with hazy yellow windows that lead to atriums of decaying leaves.

What I remember most about it was grilled cheese.

They ordered lunch for us and I was nine and only liked grilled cheese and it was as if grilled cheese was gold. For some reason, it was impossible for them to find one. It was so difficult that by the time I did get my grilled cheese it was a hunk of crusty, almost rock-hard french bread with half-melted cheddar flopping out the sides. But still, I thanked them and swallowed each bite in shards.

That was the first time I ever made money. One hundred dollars. I framed that one-hundred-dollar bill and hung it up on my wall. It stayed there for almost ten years. I can't remember what I spent it on, but I can tell you, I wish I still had that hundred-dollar bill. With the bill was a note. A note I still have tucked away in a box, ---amongst old photos, playbills, a lock of my hair wrapped in a blue and purple string from a trip to Disney World--- from the first director I ever worked with.

A thank you, signed: Josh.

The Dancers

At recess, we played double dutch,
the hard plastic hit the burning
pavement in tune. We'd run around,
gossip about the boys we liked and I'd
sit and watch as the girls I desperately
wanted to play with practiced their dance
for the talent show. I'd cheer for them,
restart their music for them and think
    this is friendship.
I'd ask them for sleepovers
and they'd say no, ask to sit at lunch
with them and they'd say no, ask to play tag
    and they'd say no.
At home, my mother would ask me
about school and I'd say it was great,
I'd beam about how much fun it all was.
At night, I'd hike up to my bedroom
    and dream of dancing too.

Audition Diaries 2

The towering building at 1515 Broadway covered the sun in a corner of Times Square. When we walked in, we're already late. The elevator brought us so high up our ears popped halfway through the ride, I clutched my glossy headshot in my hand. The doors opened and the walls were painted with neon green dripping slime, and orange splats make it all look 3D. The Nickelodeon studio was professionally cartoonish. If that's even somehow possible. The cubicles were white, organized, and boxed everyone off from each other and still, decals of SpongeBob and Timmy Turner stuck smiles onto every wall. I waited, my palm sweat all over my overexposed, photo-retouched face, in an electric blue bubble chair as they decided if they even still had time for me. I walked into a booth; the walls padded for soundproofing. This was unlike any audition I had ever been on. There was no script beforehand. No time to sit in my bed, practice to the curtains. When I was in there, the distance between me and the infamous table of furrowed browed white men felt like miles. He told me, *we're going to read you the line, then you repeat it back to me.* He read the line. My young acting nerves surged and I had to not only remember what he just said but also...act. I had to internalize the words, understand them in reference to the small character description they just gave me, and force my inflection to make something come alive. This is all to say, I couldn't remember the lines as they were read to me. I left feeling terrible and I even think I cried on the way home. I am no stranger to failure, and I wasn't then either. But still, it was like I had ruined something I would never get back, something bigger than myself.

The Tenth Audition
Brooklyn, New York,
Sometime in 2006

The woman tells me to say the words
with *more. More...something...just more.*
At age nine I know what *more* means
in the office of a CBS casting director.
I have been trained in my Saturday 9 am acting class
that *more* means furrowed brow. Eye contact: pupil deep.
Her dust-coated IKEA shelf holds a slew
of Emmy awards, glistening in low watt lamplight.
A pen twitches between her fingers,
she presses it to her lips, arranges the script in front of her.
Gary and I have practiced the sixteen words
I am here to say on the sticky seats of a Metro North train.
I drop the page to hip level so she sees me...*more*.
The Saturday morning mantras play in the curves
of my hippocampus, and the Ellery parts of me dissolve
into the kiss of my shoulder blades as I sit taller.
I have been trained to be aware of how a camera catches
everything. Every twitch of lip, scrunch of nose
every move of eye. In this moment, as I read
the words of a page-written young girl, I am eldest daughter
of Lily and Holden, in a made-up town in Illinois.

When it's over, she leans forward in her sunken leather
chair, the light that has held her haloed, floods the room,
she opens the door, and the young girl's words stay
hiding in my mouth, ready to be familiar.
I leave like I have left all auditions,
holding Gary's hand while I twirl
down the gum-stuck concrete sidewalks
of some Burrough I don't know.
On the subway ride back
to the constellation-ceilinged terminal,
he answers a call. I can hear the voice
of the halo woman through the flip phone.

ACT II

Drive to the E 14th Street Building

At 5 am I wipe the sounds
of my father's alarm clock
out my eyes, pat down
my morning hair, with half-shaded
lids I lay down in the back seat
of his gold, red-pinstriped Honda.

As we drive, I fall asleep to the sound
of air squeezing through a small crack
in the back seat window. When I wake up,
the sun hovers atop the George Washington bridge.

For a moment, the Hudson River moves
in sparkled ripples meeting the dead
debris still rooted near the highway.

It looks beautiful like this. As if,
there aren't midtown manholes
volcanizing hot steam in summer,
bags of studio apartment trash piling
up on sidewalks in Tribeca.

I stretch up to the sound of my father
swearing at potholes. I sit up and seatbelt in,
letting my duvet swallow me as I sit on the throne
of the middle seat. My father points out pigeons
and talks about how they're all going to work too.

> I love waking up and laughing with him.
> How our laughs are related, both filling
> the car with nasally shrieks. In the cloud of laughter
> it feels as if this is what our whole lives will be like.
> We will watch every sunrise together, every day, the same
> ball of fire scales the sky and we will feel its heat on
> the round of our cheekbones.

When I reach forward, my seatbelt
catches my collarbone, but if I try hard enough, pull slack
on the belt I can touch his arm. Its warmth, like the crest of sunrise,
rolling over Brooklyn's bricked skyline. I can feel the cotton of his t-shirt,

                                     his calloused hand in mine.

Natalie Snyder is:

prop. She has no defining traits other than she loves her mother and father. 'Child in the room' built to cross stage right then disappear up the staircase or behind a living room backdrop. How to stay silent. How to hold her breath so the hovering boom wouldn't hear her, how to be so unseen someone will wonder if she was ever there to begin with.

Natalie is the result of another
  storyline,
Child born from foam-cushioned-belly.
She is proof there is family. Proof
there is something watching the
tangled mess of a fifty-year
storyline.

She knows father: Holden
Mother: Lily
Sister: Faith
and brothers: Ethan and Luke

She knows how to exit when told, how
to enter, and eavesdrop. How to
pretend the doors can really lead to
another room. She does not know the
soap opera world unfolding around her.

Who her parents are cheating on each
other with, what pills her mother is
taking, who is coming back to life at
whose wedding.

She and I, the same small child together.

Where the Stairs Go

I have hidden behind the latch door; on the three
steps of the fake staircase leading from the kitchen to
the hallows behind the three-walled world. There, on
the accordion blue wall are vulgar sharpie drawings,
S-H-I-T, and other words I know from behind a slide at recess.
I wait there. Wait to hear my cue muffled through the door.
Some arguments need an interrupting child, some school attended,
some breakfast eaten. Sometimes it feels like hours. It is dark behind that door.
It is like a world of its own. I always imagine no one knows.
That those at home really think the stairs lead somewhere too.
When I break through, the studio lights hit my face
like sun, and that kitchen becomes the only one I have ever known.
A director's voice bellows *cut* and I climb the small staircase
again, and stand behind the door,   waiting.

Food on Set

sometimes, is real. In the middle of plastic Jell-O
topped with the stiff foam of supposed-to-be whipped cream,
that glisten with resin air pockets in the back of every diner
    set-piece,
is eight-hour-old food that makes this world look real.
Eating cold and sogged french fries proves to whomever
is watching CBS at 2 pm that we are human too.

                  Bits of cherry pie, sugar stuck to a ceramic plate
                  I am not supposed to clink against, but do
                  during Thanksgiving. The day my
                  TV brother learns to walk again
                  I am there, eyes sweeping the room,
                  slowly flaking pieces of a dinner roll
                                  into my mouth.

In the kitchen, wooden eggs
stay stocked in the fridge for fifty years.
the drawers of the counter don't hold
knives, or forks, or spoons, but scripts.
Scripts in the butter dish, scripts under the sink,
in between couch cushions, scripts can hide
for years in the freezer, *as the world kept turning*.

        Once, as my TV parents fight
                across the dining table during breakfast,
                the cold, pulp-swirling orange juice
                beaming bright orange. And I, young
                and thirsty, palm the glass with both hands,
                sip slowly, silently, relishing. Before the glass
                could meet the table again, the booming
                sound of a guttural *CUT* from the throat
                of the director fills the set.

Her fingers
running through the short curls of her hair,
her belt of walkie-talkies, pens, and highlighters
shaking on her hip as her face grows red. Her hands hit the table,
vibrating each grain of wood, and the orange juice ripples, I reach
forward to save it. At this moment, I think I am ten and fired.

Subway Grease

The hollow hot air, the smell of oil from the subway
is caffeine for me. It is its own kind of alarm clock.
We make it to Grand Central as the sun rises over the city,
briefcases swing from the clutches of bustling businessmen
with neckties flag-waving beneath the constellation ceiling.

I never know how we get to Brooklyn, which jerking subway
 we will take,
which way is up, which is down, which number or letter we
 take to get there.
Gary holds my hand, navigates me around the tunnels until I
 leap over
the gap into the shaking car, and yes, stand clear of the closing
 doors.
But I do know when the subway chugged out from the
 darkness
of the underground tunnel and up over the Brooklyn Bridge,
the city is beautiful. It is sun-kissed and from here, the skyline
moves like a reel of old film, filtered through the scraped,
dusted subway windows.

I swing from the overhead railing of a mostly empty subway car
like it is a greasy jungle gym, letting my feet kick in rambunctious
fashion all the way to Brooklyn. It is a stage for me.
Here, I can just be a kid. I can talk without having to follow a script.
I can be loud and run around and even leave my hair unbrushed if I want.
There are no cameras, no red recording lights, no shushing or hiding behind doors.
Just my young hands, germ-infested from the subways' many
recurring characters, and Natalie's voice,
sinking deeper into my mind.   Almost forgotten.

The Haircut

I think her name was Theresa. The woman in the hair department whose hair was hairspray-ed high in black curls while she smacked gum and says things like *darlin'*
while she fluffed my 5 am hairdo. I remember her clothed in New Jersey cheetah print, almost cartoonish in my memory, maybe with bedazzled thin flared glasses.

One of my first days in the studio, she sat me in the swivel chair pumped high so I couldn't reach the ground and draped a black cape over me. "We're gonna cut today, is that okay with dad?" She said, looking at my father who leaned against the doorframe.

"That's something we'd have to ask her mother," my father fished his flip phone out of the deep pocket of his jeans.

"Well, we're just gonna go ahead and do it then," Theresa winked at me in the mirror. I didn't care about my hair. I hated having to do anything to it, normally just pushing it out of my face with my sticky child palms. I told my mom once I'd like to just shave it off. She said I'd learn to love it.

We still have this conversation.

Theresa held a pair of scissors to the split ends sweeping my collarbones. She paused, let the blades hang just under my ears. As if my hair had been put on trial, now to be guillotined by stainless steel blades and it was time for their last words. As I collected in strands on the

black and red-tiled floor, my father, leaning half out the doorway, worries my mother won't like it.

Which he had reason to.

Theresa stepped back and styled it so the ends flip under, "When are you on set?" She asked me as she smoothed my flyways with hairspray.

"I have blocking at 2:30 they told me," I said as I pursed my lips and closed my eyes to avoid her spraying.

She looked up at the clock as she held the ends of my hair making sure each side was even. "Hmm...okay. Come back after that before you go to set."

I hopped out of the seat and continued with my Nintendo DS: Mario Kart and Super Mario Bros. Then it was time for wardrobe and blocking then down to set. I swung around the doorframe and Theresa was braiding someone's hair.

"Hi," I wave in the doorway, beaming.

"Looks good kid, you're all set." She came over to me, crouched down with a thick can of hairspray, and locked my now static-y hair into place. "Okay! I'll see you down there," Her hips swung as she moved back to her braiding.

So, I heaved open the padded doors, walked on set and the world began.

The next day, in my fifth-grade science class, one of the dancing girls passed me a note. I unfolded the creases of the scrap of lined paper.

Written, in her perfect, bubbly handwriting was: *You look like a boy.*

Dressing Rooms

Every morning, a man stuffed
behind a desk, dangles a key
in front of me. Its chain, slithering,
attached to a wooden block with a number.
Sometimes in the coldest wing, sometimes
nestled next to the green room, sometimes
perched up on the third floor, is my dressing room.
A dressing room. No matter where in the building,
the room is always the color you know was once
white. Splotches of yellow creep from the bottom seam.
The mattress is always empty, a flower-patterned sheetrock.
The desk bordered in cloudy vanity lights sometimes has real
family portraits tucked in their corners. The children's faces
 curling
that the edges and their wide smiles, so real and unpracticed.
These rooms are never mine. They are always the extra rooms,
bare and never cleaned enough. My father wraps himself
in the duvet I trekked from Connecticut, and I pop a cartridge
into my pink Nintendo DS, roam the halls, and peek
into dressing rooms that do belong to people.
I admire their sectional couches, the minifridge
they fit in there, and think about wanting to be
so important, I'll have a room to show for it.

Wardrobe

Next to a long hallway lined with Zappos shoe boxes,
the room opens its unhinged jaw to its three-story belly:
decades of clothing sweeping the floor. Plastic covered
suit jackets with long, sharp lapels, wedding dresses with
puffed sleeves pushing against their covers.

When all the other kids are there, we set our
bedazzled iPods down and push through
the shrieking hangers. We laugh at
how anything can be so old,
so swirly, so buttoned, ruffled, or tulled.

We stumble out from behind a thick rack of jackets
and our outfits are hung on a rack. An ensemble
of pink and blue plaid Bermuda shorts, tees
with lettuce trimming. Shoes, never worn, crisp
white with sparkling pink laces. I disappear
behind a curtain, switch my car-slept pajamas
with whatever pattern-mixed outfit awaited me, and stand

in front of the mirror. Twirl to the one behind and watch
all my reflections dance, spin, and stretch
                              so I can go on forever.

Three Walled World

The Many Mothers

When Natalie's mother leaves for rehab,
at the end of a season, she comes back
a new woman. This woman has hair more
chestnut, cheekbones that hill
above the square of her jaw.
This woman is a new mother.
She is not the red-nail-polished,
child-bearing-hipped woman
Natalie has always known.　　　　And　　still,

the prop enters from behind the empty hallway.
Steps over thick snake camera wire to enter
the living room, and hugs this new Lily
as she has done for all years I have been her.

The Dollhouse
Aired: 12/21/2007

It's supposed to be December
as TV grandmother, TV sister and I walk
with linked arms through the small
patch of pretend outdoors. Fake snow
is sprawled in footsteps on the plastic sidewalk.
I am in a knitted hat, a gorgeous wool coat
with buttons up the side. My hair is
flipped at my shoulders. A group
of carolers mouth Christmas song words
suited in thick, winter costumes
in front of a flat storefront with doorknobs
that don't turn. The lights beam from the rafters,
booms hover above us as we take small steps
towards a dollhouse. Lit up behind plexiglass.
> `It's a family,` TV sister says as we scan the dolls
> for faces we know.
> `Yeah, almost like ours. See?`

The practiced words leave my mouth as I point
to a doll, perched with her matching family in the living room.
She does, the doll, look like me.
And the other plastic people look like the rest of my TV family.
> `Who's to say it isn't?`

TV grandmother puts a hand
on my shoulder as I stare at the snow-crusted
roof of the dollhouse. I look up at her, hold her brown eyes
as I feel a camera inching towards my back.

Then, we cut. We wrap the scene and I child-run
to hair and makeup where they curl my hair
and pin it away from my face with a bow,
so impossibly perfectly tied so I won't touch it.
Pink my face with rouge and the wardrobe women
give me a dress. It is brown with small pink flowers
surrounding the ruched white fabric on the chest.
A pink sash holds my waist and tulle billows out
from underneath. My tights are white and my Mary Janes
hit the ground deftly as I doll walk around the studio.
I twirl around the hallways as the whole cast is fitted
in clothing from a time period I do not know exists.
When the light turns red, the rest of my made-up family
   joins me
in the living room. A Christmas tree is tall and wide,
the lights are off, but there. Hollow packages sit
bowed and glistening beneath the boughs. And we are all
the dolls in the window. At this point, it is the most beautiful
I have ever felt.

> My elbows start to stiffen, my fingers mold together,
>   my eyes, stare blankly at my TV sister staring back at me
> until
>   they no longer desire blinking. We are all just as plastic,
>   just as cold,
>   just as empty
>   as we have ever been.

We cut and before we all disperse into the darkness
of the studio, I ask the carolers
    "Why weren't you really singing?"
A woman tells me, as she removes her themed bonnet
and hands the empty sheet music to a man with a clipboard:
    "They'll put it in during post."
She walks down, passed the kitchen, the living room, the diner,
the woods of Oakdale, Illinois and I hear the high pitch of
Carol Of The Bells ring
                between the curls of my hair
                the whole way home.

Green Room

Tucked away at the end of the second-floor hallway,
its lights are always off. Lit by the low glow of a soda machine,
the insides of a clear fridge collect crisp and crusted
leftovers someone must have left there months ago. The beam
of a bubble-shaped television set in News 12 purgatory hovers
   in a corner.
Thumbtacked to wall: a Chinese New Year calendar, where we
   can tell
each other how much like the rat we are. Home of the green
   pleather couch,
peeling at the arms, the back with deep creases in the seats.
Foam exposed and squeaked when we sit. The white-haired
   hairdresser
watches as I wander in there each morning, face bright
from the screen of my Nintendo.   *Bagel? Hot Chocolate?*
She asks me. She guillotines a bagel from the platter
on a counter, lets the ticking of the toaster oven fill the room.

Peels open a packet of powdered chocolate mix, lets the hot
   water run from the
water cooler and stirs the two together. She hands me a paper
   plate
with the bagel, blonde toasted with harshly spread cream
   cheese,
the hot paper cup with coco teetering at the lip. She leaves,
say she will see me soon. And I sit, balancing the breakfast
on my small thighs and listen   to the quiet voice of the
                                                television.

The Brat and Her Brother

When the cameras stop rolling, everyone stands in the alley of settings and low hanging lights. And there, my TV brother always calls me a brat. Nearly every chance he gets.
    Brat.
        Brat.
    Brat.
Not said because he has to, not written down anywhere but because
he wants to. Because he means it.

When I say *Who comes up with these names?*
Whenever we are given a prop cereal, a board game
named so closely to its branded original. Like when we play
'Excuse Me'; named after its apologetic copyrighted
cousin.   Brat.

When I comment on how cold the diner set food is.
Brat.
When I say my costume is uncomfortable,
    out of early 2000's fashion.   Brat.

Maybe it is all in good fun. Maybe it is a peek into what having
an older brother is like in the real world. Still, he twenty-seven
   and me, ten
and unknowing of brothers, it feels like he is noticing
   something
in me that other people probably chalk up to young-ness.

When I have to sit on his knee,
the day they pig-tail my hair
and I wear pink-flowered pajamas,
I think my ten-year-old body will crush him.

So, I hover; feeling the tension in my legs grow
with each take. Two inches from my face he tells Natalie
his scripted words,

>   In a couple of years, you are going
>   to be the meanest kid there ever was.

I always wonder if he relished that moment.
If he believed it. And if he'd be happy, or unsurprised
to learn that I did grow up to be just that.
Grew up and spat back at my mother, my friends.
Grew up and blurred the lines between where that
fourth wall really ended, started, existed or didn't.
Part of me wants to believe I grew out of that shell.
That I no longer let words drape out of my mouth.
No longer hold onto 'brat' or the thought

> I am anyone else, could be anyone else
> If I will it to be so.

Three Walled World

On Lying

It was in the lunchroom. I brought a red drawstring bag to school. I got it at a charity event I had just gone to. Where soap stars rolled bowling balls with each other and some things were auctioned off. "Where'd you get that from?" A girl pulled the bag from my shoulder.

"A charity thing I went to." I pulled the bag closer to me and stared down at my cold lunch.

"No, it's not, this says *stars* on it," she snickered while the other little 11-year-olds leaned their flat ironed hair forward.

"Well, I was there, so…I'm not sure what you want me to say." I counted the speckles on the cafeteria tiles, watched as they spun, focusing my eyes on them.

"Say that you're lying, because you are."

"But I'm not lying."

"You are lying, everyone knows you lie about being on TV."

A year before, a different girl told me I was lying when I said she made me upset. Said she couldn't trust what I was saying because I was *just acting*. I tried to keep the three walls where they belonged, with their arms open on a stage in New York City. But here, in a lunchroom in Connecticut, I could feel the barriers pushing in on me.

Rooms became smaller and smaller and my voice began to practice its own lines for these comments. I wrote my own script, a day-to-day script to prove I wasn't a character; that I wasn't pretending.

Intermission

The Seven Things My Father Is

My father is a racecar driver first. Our basement, full of bubble-shaped helmets, old, creased racing suits, tools, and tools, and tools. And, of course, the smell of motor oil. We always called his car the Piloto. So much so, that he bought about 'Pilot' decal and fastened the 'o' on the end of his. Making it forever, the Honda Piloto. My father is a racecar driver first, and a business owner second. Bracecraft. LLC. His own garage full of racecars, gutted, suspended, waiting for his black, oil crusted hands to fix.

I spent a lot of time there. I'd walk through the doors with a broken toy, and my father would lift me high above his head, his smile, wide and spotlighted. He'd hold me on his hip, place my broken plastic plaything on his toolbox and he'd show me how to use a screwdriver. How to turn the small bolts, take it all apart and put it back together again. He'd take me out to the parking lot, let me hold on tight to his waist as he puttered us around on a light blue moped.

He'd let me sit in the hollowed-out shells of racecars and point to all the parts that make it work. It was all beautiful. To see someone think everything that is broken can be fixed somehow.

In the summers we'd travel to car shows. Peruse the rows of candy-apple cars, the old ones with tall wheels and cylinder bodies, trucks with doors that would come right off. Once, my father lifted me into the passenger seat of a car so perfectly red with swooping curves, driving us ever so slowly through the field. That's the closest I've ever felt to being a movie star.

Soon, he would be working on cars that were all this same shade of red. Ralph Lauren had hired him to be the curator of his car collection out in Montauk, Long Island. The very end of the island. Lauren put my father up in a home out there, with bunk beds for my sister and I, right on the beach with a small backyard. My mother said it felt like being a single parent most of the time. And I know now how it was tough for her to have her husband always be a ferry ride away.

My father is a racecar driver first, a business owner second, and a kid in a candy store third. When he opened the iron gate where Lauren's garages were; an orchard of ripe, red cars stood before us. Each one looked the same to me, and yet my father walked down the row with my sister on his hip to point out how special each one was. We'd ooh and aah at each one, my mother would hold my sticky fingers back from touching something so expensive. *Go ahead,* my father would say and my mother smiled and crouched down to touch the smooth side of the car with me.

My father is a racecar driver first, a business owner second, a kid in a candy store third, and an alcoholic fourth. In January of 2009, the car was packed and my mother was waiting for us in New Hampshire for that season's ski trip. My father, after being locked in his room for three hours, started to drive us. My sister and I buckled in, anxious to begin the long drive.

It was late when we get to New Hampshire and the roads were narrow with walls of snow beside them. Then, the sound. The slight crunch of metal as the gold, red-pinstripe Honda Piloto hit the bank on a curve.

I remember getting out of the car, scooping snow from the tires while my hands got beet red in the darkness. My father screamed from the front for me to get back in. He started waving his arms, searching for someone to stop. The roads were empty. A river of headlights spilled around the corner and a black pick-up truck stopped. In all the flurry, red and blue lights filled the night and I thought *savior*. I thought they'd pull the car out and I'd get to see my mom soon and all of this will be over. An officer swung up the door where my sister and I cowered together and asked us if we knew our father was drunk. I was eleven and *drunk* wasn't something I knew yet. The man took us back to his car. We slid into the plastic seats.

We waited, played i-Spy for two hours in the lobby of the police station until our father emerged. His fingertips black from ink and an officer closely behind him. Once again, in the back of a police car, we were taken to a hotel. At the front desk they gave us cookies while my father checked us in. In the room he called my mother. A slip on the nightstand read,

Honda Piloto pulled over.
Driving. Drunk. Two children.

My father is a racecar driver first, a business owner second, a kid in a candy store third, an alcoholic fourth, and a stranger fifth. In the months after the snowbank, my father moved in with his father in Hartford. Once a week he came back home so we could play backgammon and hug him and laugh and watch movies and eat dinner in silence. At night, he tucked us into bed, told us he loved us and I listened to his car pull out of the driveway while I prayed to a God I never believed in for him to get better. For him to come home and stay home.

My father is a racecar driver first, a business owner second, a kid in a candy store third, an alcoholic fourth, a stranger fifth, and the only thing I keep searching for sixth. On a day in early April, my mother picked us up from school and through the side door of our home, my extended family huddled in the kitchen. I walked through, threw my backpack down and smiled at everyone, *what is this? A Holiday?!* I asked. We were ushered into the living room and my uncle instructed us to hold each other's hand and bow our heads. He addresses his Lord, and I thought *this is it. My father has gone to jail.*

My mother, down on her knees before us, told us he never woke up. My father. Dead in his sleep. My nine-year-old sister fell into my mother's arms while I felt my face go red and all I could see was the carpet. Its swirling design, caterpillared along the floor. And my grandmother's hand on my shoulder as she told me how strong I was for not crying.

For years I wondered why, I wondered how. At just eleven, I held two death certificates. One, claimed accident. Alcohol and sleeping pills. The other, undetermined.

I couldn't decide which one was easier to believe.

My father was a racecar driver first. A business owner second. A kid in a candy store third. An alcoholic fourth. A stranger fifth. The only thing I keep searching for sixth.

And seventh, the only thing he can be now: dead.

Act III

Answers to Questions I Never Had

I returned to school on my birthday. My 12th birthday. I traded P.E. classes for in-school therapy and drew stick figure drawings of my family for a blubbering woman every afternoon. In that same cafeteria, with cold cut sandwiches drooping on our trays, a girl asked if she could say the word *dad* around me. I sometimes forget other people have fathers.

After my father died, Brooklyn stopped calling. They found a new Natalie and shortly after the show ended altogether and all of Oakdale, Illinois fell like dominos. Going to auditions, going to sets, those were the things my father and I did together. When I lost him, when I lost Natalie, I couldn't find my stage again.

My mother tried to send us to therapy. I'd sit around with other twelve-year-olds who had watched their parents dwindle away from some disease or another. And at the end of it, we'd eat pizza and hold hands to sing *Lean on Me*. That's how I found out my father was addicted to alcohol. In therapy. Still, the death certificate read undetermined, and I made up stories that I could hold on to for some kind of explanation.

I had been trained how to be other people for so long, that it became harder and harder to feel my own emotions. Eventually, I just let myself succumb to the nothingness. I moved through high school like a ghost, like a shell with wisps of air propelling it forward. Even now, I have flashes of memories. The years are difficult to line up, the moments are hard to place myself in and I think about everything I've done that I can't remember doing. Things I've said from the mouth I did not know, the places my legs have traveled without even knowing the body they are attached to.

I grieved again on Christmas in 2015 when I was eighteen. At dinner with my father's siblings. My aunt, her curls hanging low, told me that my father killed himself. The snowbank, the arrest, April 8th was his court date. And she told me of his wedding ring. Spinning in the bottom of a vodka bottle.

How to Come Back to Life

On August 17th, 2009, Natalie's father dies.
                                          A car crash.
With his mangled truck, bent license plate,
they found his watch.   Light brown leather hanging
              from a silver face.

Faith cries into Lily's arms. Watching this episode now, I know
   it's good I wasn't there for that.
How many fathers can I grieve?
        The soap opera world continues,
        the story lines get thicker and
        love triangles turn to hexagons.
Someone is always running away from something, from
   someone.
Six months later,   Holden is alive again.

I wish, still, that my father is alive.
>	That the body is somehow not his
and he will walk through the front door one day too.
I used to think it'd be better if he did just go to jail, or left us,
because he'd still be out there somewhere, thinking of us.
>	Because he still could. The phone would ring
and his voice would smile through the phone.
I would hug him and smell the motor oil on his shirt and
>	>	>	he would be alive.

On the day of his funeral, his body purpling grey
in his satin-cushioned casket, I think if I touch him
he will come to life again. He will sit up and breathe
and we can walk out of there together, watching the bouquets
>	>	>	>	wilt.

These things don't happen outside of the three walls.
>	There, nothing is real, anything can happen.
>	Still, we pretend that they were.
A daughter can see her dead father again,
>	and hug him.
>	He can tell her
>	>	he will never leave her.

I Remember the Years After like Falling

I can feel everything moving around me,
but I, my body, just soaring, eyes closed waiting
to hit the bottom of something. I do not know how
character I am in my own life. How prop I am to myself.
How to break from the parts of my brain that sing
acting-class-mantras of self-suppression.
I spend nearly ten years learning how to nestle
myself into the recess of a mind that has never known
who it is to begin with. Have forgotten who the self is
supposed to be. Until my name sounds like an old friend
that I always think about writing a letter to, but dont
because they have probably forgotten me.
When I look around at the spinning world around me,
I recognize nothing. I try to feel the ridges of a brick wall,
but can't. It's like floating in a fog so thick it feels like
this is just how the world really looks.
Grey and blurred at all its edges.
But I feel nothing. I have no idea how empty I am.

I know I was there, there are photos to prove that. When I do
remember, I can see the moments in my head. I am hovering
   over myself, leaning
over my own shoulder, ready to *cut, take two*, at any moment.
I became a pool of melted people.
Cresting in River-Styx-fashion.
Where no one that lives inside this body is real.
Just endless threads of learned mannerisms and memorized
   lines
trying to make something that knows how to cry on demand.
I want to watch my body be broken bones.
I imagine holding onto the banister, my feet half
over the end of the balcony, cold, sweaty palms slipping
with will I don't know I have left. Shoulder blades kissing,
my arms stretched so I look like a woman
carved into the front of a ship. Be blood staining concrete
under a balcony. I want to be eyes open, brain seeping
out of ears while my mother holds me crying. Because I believe
my bones will build new marrow, they will inch to find
connective tissue webbing together as if I was a ragdoll,
being sewn at the joints for production. Then, blood will drink
back into my body and I will be alive again.

The Dream
Where I Drown

TV mother is driving,   which is odd.
How can I still hear her soft voice say my real name?
Like we know each other. Like we are a kind of family.
She's driving us in a van-like-plane-like hybrid.
There's a child in the back seat with me, she says is her
    daughter.
               Not daughter like me. Real daughter.

Ahead, I can see the road ends in a loop, a colorful carnival
rollercoaster. I beg her to pull over, to let me out.
I don't do well on things that flip over. The car speeds
through the curve and the sun is right on my face, I am holding
    the daughter.
Holding her like she is real, like I am real and we have lives that
    can be lost.

I don't scream. I breathe deep because I know below us is
    water,
saturated blue. The kind of blue I wish the whole world
    could be.
When the car starts to sink beneath froth of the splash,
                I prepare to die.
Drowning feels like the shriveling of lungs.
Like they were never there to begin with and my body
is trying to breathe through whatever organ I have left.

I tell my mother I love her.
Not TV mother, her face has turned to salt and pepper static.
My mother, in a world barely more real than this one.

I shout to the sky, cloudless and clear as the water
I am now swallowing, for my mother.
                I am still alive.
I make my throat say *I love you* one last time.
                I am still dying.
The car hits the sanded bottom of whatever body of water
we have found ourselves sinking into and the
        bright blue fades to blinking black.

The Feeling of Things

My junior year of high school my mother said she'd pay me $20 if I auditioned for the winter play at school. Groaning and rolling my eyes I told her, "Mom," drawing out the oooo sound, "I don't know, my schedule, you know I don't know if I can do it."

"But you used to love it," she said as she put a hand on my shoulder.

"I know, but it's just not *cool*."

"Cool? Oh, you're worried about being *cool*." Her gaze slid away from me as she ended our conversation.

In high school I was so worried about being "cool." I wanted to be like the girls that walk down the halls in slow motion, have the same grip they somehow had over their student body. I watched a lot of movies like that. Of cool girls, their football boyfriends, and the parties they'd go to and how happy they all were because of those things. I wanted to be that. So, fourteen-year-old me created that person.

I made out under stairways, I got half-drunk at parties, had sex, and smoked things I said I never would. I felt nothing.

I cried when I lost my virginity. Because it was gone? Because it was something that someone had made up that I had lost, that a boy had claimed it from me? Maybe it was because that summer, huddled on a bottom bunk at summer camp a girl told me when she did it, and her 'cherry' popped. It was like that scene from *The Shining*. She told me how bad it hurt. I thought sex was this horrible blood bath of pain. And when I did it, it didn't hurt at all. There was no blood, there was no ripping pain. There was nothing. I felt nothing. I think that's why I cried.

One day, in art class, my football playing boyfriend stood in the doorway. *Get out here*, he said to me. We spent the next twenty, thirty, I don't know how many minutes fighting up and down the halls. Calling each other names, screaming about things I can't even remember. And crying, so much crying, tucked behind lockers we used to kiss in front of. The one thing I remember, and I'll never forget this, he said, "No one can ever earn you." The words ring like bells inside my head even now. And I was there crying to a sixteen-year-old boy in shock.

No one can ever earn you. No *one* can ever earn you. No one can ever *earn* you. No one can ever earn *you*.

I carried those words with me for years. I let them be real as I continued to make choices I can't remember making. And in the trunk of a car, when a boy held me by the throat and said, "you like it, whore, you like it," when I was seventeen, I thought of those words then.

In winter, I took my mom up on her $20 offer. I walked into the audition room, recited a poem I had a written down from a performance I saw on YouTube. The last lines of that poem were "You're. So. Beautiful." And the director said, "and you are." And I was cast in that play. It's one of my only, real memories of high school. I remember being so happy. Being so comfortable and I could feel that crooked stage below me. And it felt so real.

My Mother

As a child I loved my mother deeply. I held her hands and waved my hands together so she would lift me. She was older when she had my sister and I and everyday she's gotten younger. It's hard to remember our first memory together. It was drip castles. Yes, making drip castles with her by the shore of Cape Cod. We'd sit just where the waves drowned the sand, pick up a fist full and let it drip from our palms as it built a sloping, sand-stacked castle. I remember that summer. My grandfather used to rent a house on the beach there. My father taught us how to fly butterfly kites and my mother chased a peanut butter and jelly stealing seagull down the beach until she pried the sandy sandwich bag from its strong beak. I remember that summer, when the sun dripped down behind the tide like sand, my mother, waddling with bags of toys and towels, fell. She fell backwards down the steep stairway leading to the house. I remember that summer because when she fell, I felt what it might have felt like to lose her. Her head, splintering the weak railing, her back hand barely catching her fall, my father, my running father, cupping the nape of her sand-crusted neck. I never thought I would feel anything like that again.

As a teenager, I never lashed out at my mother. I couldn't. Our fridge was full of casserole condolences for months and the house already hung heavy for years after. She let me make my own mistakes. I'd do my own hair, bangs, two centimeters long. I'd dye my hair, bleach it, dye it again and she'd stroke my dead ends and pray it'd grew back. I did, however, lie to my mother. Mostly about where I was going. I'd say we were going to Amanda's when really, we were at a party at Lewis' where two girls had to get their stomachs pumped. Sneaking out was hard, but I did it. I'd wait near the door, cough to cover the creek of the screen door and slip through the smallest opening I could. I never believed I was in any real danger, and she knew that I knew if I was, I could call her. I like to believe now, my mother trusted me. At sixteen she sat me down and told me all about alcohol and one day I was going to drink it and I could get addicted to it, it's just in my Capshaw blood. When she told me this, I had already tried lemon vodka getting ready for homecoming.

As an adult, I call my mom every day. Sometimes twice a day. We tell each other we love to hear the other's voice. There are so many things I want to ask her. But I don't. I've seen her cry too many times. I tell her about the groceries I bought, that apples were on sale that day. She asks me what I'm doing on the weekend and most of the time I say nothing. And she says *that's nice* but I really think she worries about me. That I'm alone and sad and crying even when we're not on the phone. Which is true. And when we hang up the call, after we say *I love you* my empty living room is just that. Empty.

On Google Searching

When I tell people for the first time, being on a
CBS soap opera for three years—
when my brain was just starting to learn long division—
becomes the only interesting thing about me.
Every time, I suddenly turn into the Google image.
The one where I am short-haired,
freckled with arms crossed in an attempt
to hide a ketchup stain. The aftermath of a mountain
of chicken tenders and fries at a charity event. I am
the website with virus-crusted pop-up ads saying I worth
700,000 dollars. I am always asked to tell stories
about what happened between the bricks
of the E 14th street building.
      And every time, I do.
I tell the stories about the bagels in the green room,
the staircase, and the places scripts would hide.
How I tumbled out of bed wrapped
in my duvet. The waking up, the sun, my father
and how alive everything seemed to be.
After sitting in the cloud of decade-old,
half-remembered moments, I hope I am enough.

How Endings are Also Beginnings

In the basement of my unairconditioned dorm building
I slate my name; my height and *I'm reading for the role of*
_____.
Holding a smile on the fifth take is always the hardest part.
I prop my iPhone on a chair, a washing machine or
a crook in the wall. And start, stop, start, stop, as I read the lines.
I panic, rush to move my camera every time a footstep sounds.
I continue acting because I was too afraid to ask to stop.
I buy a 2010 Honda with my *As The World Turns* money
like my father's. I don't want to do it anymore. I know I am seeing the
world as if everything is three-walled and hollow but don't know
how to get out of it. I don't know if I can. So, I read lines, I memorize
monologues and I inevitably transfer schools to be an acting major.

I cry during that audition. They aren't going to let me in. I already
have two years of college done and they don't think I can handle it.
So, I cry. Hysterically. I beg. Plead. I need to get out of where I am.
I need to get out. I do, and I drop the acting major. And on a Saturday,
at a football game with a hundred thousand other blue and white clad fans,
I feel the cord at the base of my brain find its socket again. I feel the ground
I am standing on; I feel each muscle stretch as I wave my arms up high.
I am back. Back in this body, and I know it to be true.

My Father, My Natalie, My Memory

I remember my father the way I remember Natalie.
A part of me that I lost, that I pull out, unfold from
my back pocket or pull out from the pages of a yellowed
book to say *here's how you know me.*

I can remember my father's voice,   its tone
like windchimes, like silver bells, rustling against
thick snow. Still beautiful. Still muffled. Still there.

I remember Natalie like any other dead thing.
I remember her eyes,   desperately trying
to say something, her movements, her words,
                                                  her life
         so planned out for her,
right there on the page. All she needed to do was   flip
to find out what happened next.
I remember Natalie the way I remember any other dead thing.
         That is to say,
                             I wish I could spend more time with her.

Even now, When I Close My Eyes, I Can See Her

Natalie stands at the top of the fake staircase and I try to climb
                         fast enough to get to her as the three stairs
                         grow and grow.
The running will never stop.
                     The stairs keep multiplying,
changing their direction,   jagged patterns. I can see her
                  rapidly ascending in

peering over the edge
             of the final stair,
                      her freshly cut blonde hair
                      dripping down.
                      Maybe she's about to fall, jump,
                      stumble into the
               suspended darkness
                             just behind the walls
where every fabricated world I have ever lived in happens.

When I reach her, Natalie hangs one foot just over the edge
   of the stairs.
The sound of hissing camera-wire-snakes vibrates somewhere
   unnamable.

What happens now, Natalie's voice echoes and fills this
void we share together. I try move my lungs but here,
there is no breath to catch. There's no air, just her
voice, ringing, fading into a sparkling distant chime.

She replants herself on the top step and turns to me.
> When she looks at me, I can't believe I was
> ever so small,
>> so freckled and unstartled. She knows
>> nothing of what will happen.
> It's 2008 here on this staircase and she knows
>   nothing.
> Not who she is, not who I am, not what's waiting
>   for her
> at the bottom of these stairs.

So much, I tell her as we sit next together on the top step.
> We run our fingers across the blue accordion
>   wallpaper,
> count the crude drawings and softly say the swear
>   words
> to ourselves for practice. And we wait. Together.

Cover Charge

I learned what mystery tasted like
at the bottom of a Pinnacle Whipped bottle.

Warm Sunset Blush Franzia
tasted like passing my driver's test,
like voting, having a credit card,
paying my own bills.

At eighteen, the burn
of strawberry lemonade Svedka
in the sweating apartment of a sorority sister
tasted like a badge I could sew into my skin.
I had earned the blackout.

Hangovers then were breakfast at noon—
chips, queso, grape soda, fries,
cheeseburgers dripping from our mouths
as we laughed through the wreckage
of what happened.

Who fell.
Who spilled.
Who gave their number to who.

It felt like a club
with an entry fee.
Cover charge.
Buy in for another hand.

There I was, in the middle of it all.
Laughing, drinking, disappearing.
My whole life pouring out
into a plastic cup.

The National Institute on Drug Abuse Says 50% of My Addiction is Genetics

Drinking alone was sacred to me. I could let bubbled
wine slip down my throat, bottle after cheap bottle
and no one knew. Like sneaking cookies from the pantry or
hiding my flip phone under the covers, drinking alone
felt dangerous.

I found myself so drunk one night, sitting on the floor,
staring into my mirror. Really looking at my face. At its bumps,
creasing valleys, how bloated I had become. I sat there
and cried. I wanted to slice around my skull and suck
out my own shrinking brain, give it back to my father. To say
here, here is what you made me.
Not in a way that I hated him, in a way that
I loved him so much that I did not want to become him.
I thought for a while I had control of my life.
That I could stop drinking if I wanted to. It wouldn't kill
me, because I was stronger than that.
Because I knew the sadness
of reading a death certificate.
I knew what yearning felt like.

How to Celebrate the Dead

Twice a year, I seek out a Mexican restaurant
with gaudy walls, sticky floors, and a menu,
a novel, with endless rounds of warm, thin,
and salted tortilla chips. A strawberry margarita
big enough to fish in, drown in, laugh in,
and remember my father. Like the place we used to go,
where the mariachi would sing to him and my sister,
my mother smiled and clapped our young hands together.
I would bite eyes and a mouth into a flour tortilla,
wear it as a mask while turning refried beans and rice
to mush. Twice a year, I try to recreate my childhood.
First, the day he died. April.
Second, his birthday. October.

For the second time this year,
I find the place. One that Yelp reviewers
deem good enough—which is exactly
what my father would have wanted.
Good enough is still half good. And still half enough.
I go alone. Wallowing while swallowing the sugared
rim of every glass, tequila like an old friend beside me.
I try to tell myself that this was the loneliness
that drove him. That feeling is all I have left.

I wonder about his favorite movie, song, moment.
My belly, full of beans, flour, and sugared sick
with fake strawberries, swells as I sit
in an empty restaurant, trying to remember
the sound of his voice, the smell of motor oil
on his t-shirts. With a knot in my throat,
I think about this poem.

Five Years and Four Days After I First Said I Needed to Stop Drinking, I Did

I was tired of the hangovers, the mental gymnastics of figuring out when I could start drinking during the week, and what I could blame Thursday night's bottle of wine on. I didn't drink *that* much, right? Just half a 1.5-liter bottle of Barefoot Sauvignon Blanc on Thursday, a full one on Friday, another half on Saturday after I'd had three glasses of wine at dinner, and half of another bottle on Sunday. I told myself it wasn't that bad. I was really only hungover once a week. I'm in my twenties—this is just what life is like.

Being 27 means headaches, bloated bellies, deep circles under the eyes, late-night food ordering, stomach cramps, and checking restaurant menus not for food, but for the cheapest glass of wine. Eyeing waiters for refills before I was halfway done. It's just wine, right? It's not like I was taking shots at the bar at 2 a.m. every day. I was just spending Monday, Tuesday, and Wednesday waiting for Thursday—when I'd be alone in my apartment, and I could put on *Mamma Mia*, drink sweet wine for dinner, dance and sing until I sweated it all out. I heard the snake say *eat the apple Eve* and I sucked it to its core. I called that freedom.

Of course, I was chained to the thin neck of a $12.79 Barefoot bottle.

I cherished the empty stomach, the first knowing buzz.

How it spread from brain to fingertip like a wave tumbling over me. The world felt less real to me when I was drunk. As if I could reach up and bend the clouds into a balloon animal or grab the sun and throw it. I used to count the days I drank and pat myself on the back when it was less than four. I could use the extra days like rollover minutes on an old cellphone plan. When I'd count and realize I drank for more days than I didn't, the earth opened like a vortex to take me in its wake. I thought about every bad thing I ever did in my life, how no good person would do this. Oh, how my head would swirl even more.

On March 17th I quit drinking. A Monday. I woke up over the toilet, heaving and hoping that whatever was making me shake would wrench itself out of me. "I need to stop drinking," I said through choking tears four days before this. Yet, there I was—another half bottle of Barefoot down, feeling like a rhetorical question asked again and again.

That morning, the most amazing man I've ever met said to me, "You have to get your shit together." He held the mirror up to me, so I could see all my bumps, creasing valleys, how bloated I had become. Though I didn't dream of the knife, or shrinking, or hiding, or disappearing.   I did something I had never done before. I meant what I had said.

When I reached one week sober, I thought I'd drink again. At two weeks, I thought for sure I had done enough. The clinking sound of glass rattled in my head. The silky taste of a crisp, cold white wine dangled like a carrot in front of me.

After a month, I stopped thinking about all the things I hadn't done and started noticing everything I had. I went to Portland, Oregon, then Seattle, Washington. I climbed to the top of Multnomah Falls. I hiked Forest Park and Mount Rainier. I went to the top of the Space Needle and feared I would fall. I connected more deeply with my relationship. I tried on sparkling diamond rings. I had more time to say yes to the things my drinking would have made me say no to. I went to a concert on a Monday night and went to work the next day. I threw a birthday party with raspberry lemonade and cupcakes. I helped my mother move. I walked at 5 am to the beach and saw the Long Island Sound wake up.

I cried more than I knew I still could.

I got my 30-day chip—red and shining—and I carry it in my pocket when I do the hard things. Hard things like

> lunch on a patio on a beautiful spring day.
> Like when my partner loses his job.
> Like when I publish a poem.
> When I go to the beach.
> At night around a fire.
> Our anniversary.
> Every Thursday night.
> When my father dies.
> When my friend's father dies.

Most of my early sobriety, I have thought of my father. The way we both hid bottles, emotions, and our struggles from everyone. Maybe in hopes that they would just go away. We could recycle them like glass. Or we could drink and drink until nothing existed. Not even ourselves. Each day, I'm glad that I do exist.
    I have the whole world ahead of me to explore—
sober, steady, and entirely here.

My Father Has Been Dead for Sixteen Years & Last Night I Dreamt it Was a Lie

As I walk through the door, he is there
playing the guitar–which he doesn't know how to do.
He says, *Let's go to Madison Square Garden.*

    Here, the guitar sounds like memory:
    blurry, faded, and beautiful.
    Here, we can do anything:
    speak, play guitar, and be alive.

He says he wants to swim. It has been so long
since he felt the water. My father dove into a lake.

    It's water, black like our touching shadows.
    And I want to beg him not to. But I don't.
    I don't tell the dead man he cannot swim.

& I wait–like a daughter– at the other side for him.
I wait for him. I wait for him the way I waited for him
to walk through the door all those years ago. I wait for so long

Three Walled World

I can feel my own heart beating.
I worry he might have died again.
I prepare for another funeral.

He emerges dry. Just as I remember. Just as he was
in the *Summer 2004* home video I cherish.
His hair, a collection of black whisps. His smile,
red with strong cheekbones. Dressed in a
loose linen half buttoned shirt; khakis held up
by a breaking belt.

>He sits with me.
>He sits with me
>and this is all I've ever wanted.

His face, an abstract painting my sleeping brain
is trying to make shapes out of.

>His voice, like magic.
>Like sand falling in an hourglass,
>Like chimes, the kind that make you
>feel whole again. Home again.

He tells me how exhausting it is to watch dreams
when you die. That he watches them through a window.
Like a child left out, like a dog watching traffic.
He tells me he knows I'm a poet.

My mother told him.
Maybe in her whispering prayers
one night, maybe in a dream,
maybe while he was still alive
and she saw the future.
Flaming, charred, and empty.

He tells me something about love and I'll lie here
and tell you he said *I love you.*

I wake to the sound of dog's collar shaking.
I open my eyes. Remember
                I am alive & cry.

Acknowledgments

I want to acknowledge my mentors both at the Pennsylvania State University and Southern Illinois University that pushed me not only to create this work but to be a poet. My colleagues that read this collection every week for three years, thank you for your time, attention, and support. Thank you to the presses that made homes for my work throughout the years, all poetry finds its way home eventually.

About the Author

Ellery Capshaw, a Connecticut native with an MFA in Creative Writing. *Three Walled World* is her debut collection. Her work as been published both online and in print. Outside of writing, she loves to explore near and far, always finding a metaphor along the way. Follow her on Instagram @ell_caps.

Also by CLASH Books

ALL OUR TOMORROWS

Amy DeBellis

AMERICAN THIGHS

Elizabeth Ellen

LOVER GIRL

Nicole Sellew

THE SNARLING GIRL

Elisa Albert

THE MISEDUCATION OF A 90s BABY

Khaholi Bailey

HOW TO GET ALONG WITHOUT ME

Kate Axelrod

WITCH HUNT & BLACK CLOUD

Juliet Escoria

EARTH ANGEL

Madeline Cash

ALL THINGS EDIBLE, RANDOM & ODD

Sheila Squillante

www.ingramcontent.com/pod-product-compliance
Lightning Source LLC
LaVergne TN
LVHW040156080526
838202LV00042B/3184